VICTORY

VICTORY

The 4 Step Process for Every Believer

Michael L. Jefferson

High Mountain
An Imprint of Righteous Road Publishing House

Unless otherwise indicated, all Scripture quotations are taken from The Message: The Bible in Contemporary Language, copyright © 2002.

Other versions are NKJV, the New King James Version of the Bible. Copyright © 1979, 1980, 1982, 1988, by Thomas Nelson, Inc., publishers.

VICTORY: T*he 4 Step Process for Every Believer*. Copyright © 2006 by Michael Jefferson. All rights reserved. Printed in the United States of America. No part of this book may be used or reproduced in any manner whatsoever without written permission except in the case of brief quotations embodied in critical articles and reviews.

Righteous Road Web Site: http://www.righteousroad.com

Righteous Road™, ™, and High Mountain™ are trademarks of Righteous Road Enterprises Inc.

ISBN 978-0-9831615-0-9

I dedicate this book to my mother,
Sharon Mary Jefferson.

Your name means "Princess." May your Father,
the King of kings, shower all His blessings upon you.

"And the mother of the child said, 'As the Lord lives, and as your soul lives, I will not leave you.' … "

2 KINGS 4:30 (NKJV)

Your love, support, and guidance
will stay with me forever.

I am so blessed to have you as my mother.

CONTENTS

INTRODUCTION **TO THE INTRODUCTION**   P09

INTRODUCTION **KNOW THE WORD**   P15

FIRST STEP **DO THE WORD**   P23

SECOND STEP **RENEW YOUR MIND**   P33

THIRD STEP **BELIEVE IN YOUR HEART**   P41

FOURTH STEP **CONFESS WITH YOUR MOUTH**   P51

EPILOGUE **BEING HONEST WITH YOURSELF**   P59

INTRODUCTION
TO THE INTRODUCTION

God blessed them:
"Prosper! Reproduce! Fill Earth! Take Charge! ..."
Genesis 1:28

I have a strong desire to see Christians truly blessed.
Michael L. Jefferson

Victory

For as long as I have lived, I have enjoyed any opportunity to be put in a position of authority because I value rules and regulations. I know what's right and wrong and I enjoy seeing justice being served. This is why I went to college to become a Family Court Judge. What better opportunity exists to dispense justice than to be a judge? The litigants would come before me and I would dispense true justice. I value justice so intensely; I know it would be dispensed. God; however called me into another arena where I would have authority.

He called me into ministry.

I accepted the call.

The call forced me to study the Word in a way I had not done before. I found God's rules and regulations to be more just and swift than any of the laws found in any country in the world. God will also ensure it is carried out. Through my studies, I have developed a stronger fellowship with Him.

Through this fellowship, I have come to find out much about God.

I found He is the God of love

He is the God of purpose.

He is the God of power.

I found that He does not lie. He gave me an assignment to inform believers of their rights and to teach them how to live in the victory that God promised in His Word. God wants His children to know that He is sincere and that He truly wants them to experience every promise in His Word. He does not want His children defeated in any way.

I thought this Word would be easily understood and carried out, yet I have found that the enemy has worked really hard for a very long time to keep Christians defeated.

Luke 10:18-19 states:

> **Jesus said, "I know. I saw Satan fall, a bolt of lightning out of the sky. See what I've given you? Safe passage as you walk on snakes and scorpions, and protection from every assault of the Enemy. No one can put a hand on you.**

Wow! Jesus has given me this authority and therefore I gladly take on the enemy while I share the Word with God's children! What a privilege indeed!

Most Christians sincerely believe in God and in Jesus, as Lord and Savior of their life, but have a problem believing that God wants them blessed in every way. These Christians read His Word, but do not understand that God's promises are for them.

Somehow, the enemy has achieved a very twisted and perverted goal: to keep the believer in a defeated life.

God wants all believers blessed! Life should be a great journey! Through the principles found in this book, you will discover that God's plan is for you to obtain victory in every arena in your life! God, Himself, will see you through! There first needs to be an understanding that the Word of God is the same as God's Will.

Through these pages, discover the life that has been waiting for you! The life God has been so desperate for you to find. The lies that the enemy has told you about God being some cruel score-keeper in the sky, keeping track of all your sins and good deeds, needs to be debunked! He is our Father!

Let me make this personal:

God is *your* Father. (1 John 3:1-3)

God is *your* Helper. (Hebrews 13:6)

God is *your* friend. (John 15:12-17)

God will never leave *you* - ever! (Hebrews 13:5)

God is quick to forgive *you* of your sins. (Psalm 86:5)

God is *your* source for all! (Genesis 22:14)

Let the journey begin!

INTRODUCTION
KNOW THE WORD

My people are ruined because they don't know what's right or true...

Hosea 4:6

Knowledge is power.

Sir Francis Bacon

Victory

The words in Hosea 4:6 reverberated in my soul when I first read it many years ago.

It shattered my view of Christianity. Up to that moment I thought Christians were immune to being ruined or destroyed.

The Bible says:

> **"... your body is the temple of the Holy Spirit who is in you, whom you have from God, and you are not your own..."**
> ~1 Corinthians 6:19, NKJV

If this is the case, what basis is there for any Christian to be ruined, or destroyed?

God reveals the answer.

"They don't know."

What is it that Christians don't know?

"The Word of God."

Not knowing the Word of God causes destruction.

This very phrase tells me that as Christians, we have an obligation to know the Word of God.

Although God created us and rescued us from the enemy, through Jesus' sacrifice, (John 3:16; John 10:10), we still have an active part to play in our lives.

We must know the Word of God because knowing the Word of God will keep us safe from the enemy's attacks. The enemy commonly attacks us through our mind by telling us lies about ourselves.

For example, the devil may say to you, "you are poor because God wants you to learn a valuable life lesson in this…" or he might say, "you are sick right now because God wants you to learn how to rely on Him more."

At this point, you may feel tempted to believe the lies and fall prey to the devil. However, knowing what the Word of God says will protect you from all of these lies.

The Bible says:

> **"So, my very dear friends, don't get thrown off course. Every desirable and beneficial gift comes out of heaven. The gifts are rivers of light cascading down from the Father of Light. There is nothing deceitful in God, nothing two-faced, nothing fickle. He brought us to life using the true Word, showing us off as the crown of all his creatures."**

~James 1:17-18

The proper way to respond to the enemy in this example is to say, "No Satan! God wants me blessed and in perfect health! You, the enemy, have brought poverty and sickness my way! Not God!"

Always respond to the enemy using the Word of God.

The Bible tells us:

> **So let God work His will in you. Yell a loud no to the Devil and watch him scamper.**
>
> ~James 4:7

Therefore, read the word.

Study the Word.

God's Word *is* God's will.

That is why it is called the "New Testament."

Be counted among those Christians who *know* what the word of God says! By knowing God's Word, you will know His will for your life. As you have seen in the last example, knowing God's will for your life will keep you from being deceived by the enemy.

However, if you do not know the Word, and the enemy brings an attack, you may fail to see it for what it is. Worse yet, you may perhaps embrace it, believing that it is from God. It is perhaps one of the enemy's most vile attacks. The devil will attempt to make the believer think these attacks are from God.

The Christian that does not know what the Word of God says may respond to an illness by saying, "The Lord has a plan for this cancer. He is trying to teach me something." In this scenario, precious time is spent pondering the lesson behind the illness instead of using the Word of God to fight it! In the end, unless natural treatment is successful, death becomes the result.

God wants us to realize how much the enemy despises us.

Jesus says:

> **"The thief does not come except to steal, and to kill, and to destroy..."**
>
> ~John 10:10, NKJV

There are four core reasons why you must first know God's Word:

1) You will find out who God is.

2) You will find out who you are.

3) You will find out what you are entitled to.

4) You will know what is expected of you.

Knowing who God is, and who He is not, will aide you powerfully on your journey through life. You will come to discover the true character and essence of our Lord! He is holy, righteous, wise, eternal and powerful!

The Bible also informs us of who we are.

The Bible says:

> **"God spoke: 'Let us make human beings in our image, make them reflecting our nature...'"**
>
> ~Genesis 1:26

We are created in God's image (we are spirits!) and we share his nature! What an astounding truth that we would have only known because we read God's Word!

As such, we are entitled to many privileges! Jesus tells us the reason He came to earth, died and resurrected, was so that we would have life in all its fullness (John 10:10).

Lastly, one of the most crucial reasons for knowing the Word is to know what God expects *of* us.

This book concentrates on what is expected of us.

Do not forget Hosea 4:6, where God tells us what happens to those Christians who fail to know His word. God expects us to use our God-given authority to walk in the freedom that is promised to us.

The Bible says:

> **"Behold, I give you the authority to trample on serpents and scorpions, and over all the power of the enemy, and nothing shall by any means hurt you."**
> ~Luke 10:19, NKJV

The Bible says:

> **"Then you will experience for yourselves the truth, and the truth will free you."**
> ~John 8:32

God expects a lot from us because He has given us so much. He has given us authority and truth. Our authority must be utilized because Jesus is sitting at the right hand of Father God (Colossians 3:1). While He is there, He gave us Christians the Holy Spirit (Galatians 3:14) while we are here on the earth. If there was no work expected of us, there would be no reason for Jesus to give us the authority or the Holy Spirit.

Knowing the truth – God's Word - will set you free!

If you do not read the Word, you will not realize that we were set free from the enemy and from sin (Romans 6:18), and sadly you will continue to live in bondage.

What's the bottom line?

Know the Word.

FIRST STEP
DO THE WORD

Don't fool yourself into thinking that
you are a listener when you are anything but,
letting the Word go in one ear and out the other.
Act on what you hear!

James 1:22

When you know better, you do better.

Maya Angelou

Victory

This is where the rubber meats the road, so to speak. Once you know what the Word says about any given situation in your life, you must *do* the Word to experience victory.

Jesus says:

> **"These words I speak to you are not incidental additions to your life, homeowner improvements to your standard of living. They are foundational words, words to build a life on. If you work these words into your life, you are like a smart carpenter who built his house on solid rock. Rain poured down, the river flooded, a tornado hit – but nothing moved that house. It was fixed on that rock. But if you just use my words in Bible studies and don't work**

> **them into your life, you are like a stupid carpenter who built his house on the sandy beach. When a storm rolled in and the waves came up, it collapsed like a house of cards."**
>
> ~Matthew 7:24-27

Notice the difference between those who hear the Word of God and those who hear *and do* the Word of God! Straight from Jesus' lips – not mine. Only those who hear and do the Word of God will be sustained in this life, and will experience the victory that God promised!

But for the person who only hears the Word, life will be tragic. This truth explains why some Christians who attend church, volunteer, etc., are still living defeated, purposeless and selfish lives.

This truth explains why there are Christians who are constantly

- ✓ sick,
- ✓ poor,
- ✓ and defeated

in every way.

The Bible says:

> **"Stay alert! Watch out for your great enemy, the devil. He prowls around like a roaring lion, looking for someone to devour."**
>
> ~1 Peter 5;8, NLT

Whom may the devil devour? The devil may devour both non-Christians and Christians who do not do the Word of God!

Both are easy prey for the devil. I picked up on something crucial in Matthew 7:24-27 that I need to share with you all.

Notice that *both* those who only hear; and those who hear and do will experience the storms of life! Both will have struggles, pains, battles, hurts, etc. in this life, but only one will be victorious.

Jesus is saying that it does not matter who you are or what you believe, you will be attacked in life. Jesus says, of the devil, "...[he] is only there to steal and kill and destroy..." (John 10:10).

Think of it, the devil is going to attempt to steal your joy, love, peace, authority, and life regardless of whether or not you do the Word.

Therefore, it would behoove you to do God's Word.

Doing God's Word promises to bring victory.

Have you ever made any of the following statements?

"I see what you are saying, but...

- ✓ I'm poor
- ✓ I'm sick
- ✓ I'm alone
- ✓ I'm depressed
- ✓ I have a horrible self-image
- ✓ I never have peace."

If you have ever said any of these statements, I have both good news and bad news for you. The bad news is that you are right. The good news is that you do not have to remain that way.

If the devil is going to attack you anyway, then it behooves you to do the Word so that you may defeat him!

Why continue to be depressed, sick, selfish, purposeless and alone if you do not have to be?

This may sound harsh, but God is not going to see your plight and respond by saying, "Oh my! Look at my child! I am going to go back on my Word and rescue them anyway.

Who cares what I said in Hosea?! I am going to get them out of there!" God will *not* go back on His Word.

The Bible says:

> **"God is not a man, that He should lie..."**
> ~Numbers 23:19, NKJV

God is no liar. When it says that His people are destroyed for lack of knowledge, it's the truth. Heed to the warnings of God! Apply His Word to your life to experience the victory *promised* by God and not the destruction *planned* by the enemy.

If you feel that you have been worn out by life's struggles, and have been left extremely weak, there is still hope for you.

Be of good cheer!

The Bible says:

> **"Satan's angel did his best to get me down; what he in fact did was push me to my knees ... [God] told me, 'My grace is enough; it's all you need. My strength comes into its own in your weakness.'"**
> ~2 Corinthians 12:7-9

God has promised *His* strength when you are weak!

Start to be victorious by praising God for who He is and your spirit will be lifted!

Search the Word for what it is you need and, then do what the Word commands you to do.

The victory comes from *doing* the Word.

It doesn't come by "hanging in there" or by "keeping on keeping on." These are religious trite phrases that do not contain any power!

The power is contained in God's Word!

The devil's whole plan is to keep you from knowing this truth. Once you push pass that obstacle, his next plan is to keep you from doing the Word. The devil knows the great power that resides in the Word of God.

God told Joshua:

> **"Don't get off track, either left or right, so as to make sure you get to where you're going. And don't for a minute let this Book of the Revelation be out of mind. Ponder and meditate on it day and night, making sure you practice everything written in it. Then you'll get to where you're going and then you'll succeed. Haven't I commanded you? Strength! Courage! Don't be timid; don't get discouraged. God, your God, is with you ever step you take."**
>
> ~Joshua 1:8-9

Again, notice that God says it is *after* you do His Word that you will get to where you are going. It is then that you will succeed. This is the established Word of God. The Word of God is the will of God. Do not let the enemy keep deceiving you about why you are in the situation you are in. The devil wants you to stay ignorant of your rights.

The devil works very hard to keep Christians discouraged. The only way he can keep you discouraged is by keeping you away from God's Word. If he can get you to doubt God, or doubt His love for you, then he can keep you in bondage and deeply discouraged. And a discouraged Christian is a defeated Christian. That is why God commands us to not be discouraged (Colossians 3:21)! This is a command from God Himself.

To be discouraged means to be deprived of:

- ✓ confidence,
- ✓ hope,
- ✓ and spirit.

God came to give us life, and the life He came to give us contains:

- ✓ confidence,
- ✓ hope,
- ✓ and spirit!

This is what the enemy has come to steal, kill and destroy. God commands us to not allow him to do so!

Therefore, if you *stay* discouraged, you are in sin. Sin, according to the Word is the transgression of the law. If you are in sin, the devil has you right where he wants you, because the wages of sin is death (Romans 6:23).

Death is the opposite of life.

And it is life that Jesus says He came to earth for you to have. Do not be fodder for the enemy! The wages of being discouraged is death.

The enemy does not want you to follow through on the Word, and to ensure that you do not, he tries to make you doubt what God's will is for your life. Let the deception end today!

God's Word is God's will for your life! Let your faith grow in order for you to do the very Word of God! Receive your promises that were bought for you with Jesus' blood!

Jesus says:

> "... **He also took the cup after supper, saying, 'This cup is the new covenant in My blood, which is shed for you...'**"
>
> ~Luke 22:20, NKJV

Always remember how much God loves you and do not forget the price He paid for you to live in victory!

SECOND STEP
RENEW YOUR MIND

... I will put My law in their minds ...

Jeremiah 31:33 (NKJV)

The devil knows that if he can capture our mind,
he holds our future.

Joe Campbell

Victory

The mind is our battleground. It is vital in the process of experiencing victory. God tells us that our mind must be renewed *daily* because it still believes the lies of the enemy. The devil is the father of lies. Unlike our spirits, our minds were not renewed upon receiving Jesus as our Lord and Savior.

The Bible says:

> **"Therefore, if anyone is in Christ, he is a new creation; old things have passed away; behold, all things have become new."**
>
> ~2 Corinthians 5:17, NKJV

God deals with us (our spirit self) directly because He is spirit (John 4:24) – and *we* are to deal with our minds and bodies. If you do not renew your mind daily, none of the new truths in the Word will do you any good. This is because your mind plays an important role of God manifesting His whole self in our lives.

The Bible says:

> **"And do not be conformed to this world, but be transformed by the renewing of your mind, that you may prove what is that good and acceptable and perfect will of God."**
>
> ~ Romans 12:2, NKJV

Wow! What a profound statement! First, we are told to not be conformed to this world.

We keep ourselves from being conformed when we transform ourselves by the renewing of our minds.

Well, what does it mean to renew the mind? How does one renew one's mind?

The way to renew your mind is to read God's perspective, will, word, commands and teachings daily. When you do this, you are renewing your mind.

For example, if you feel alone in this world, read God's perspective.

God's Word is God's perspective.

In your bible, find out what God says about your loneliness.

The Bible says:

> **"…He's right there with you. He won't let you down; he won't leave you."**
>
> ~Deuteronomy 31:6

Once you find this scripture, read it over and over until it sinks in. Then, throughout your day, and especially at times when you feel most alone, think of God's perspective.

Continue to tell yourself that God will not leave you. He will not let you down. Think of this whenever you begin to feel alone, where you normally would have thought to yourself, "I am so alone."

Do this repeatedly, as to not allow your mind to wander off course. Think to yourself, "God is right here with me. He will not let me down. He will not leave me." As you do this, you are renewing your mind, on your way to transformation!

Remember:

> **"And do not be conformed to this world, but be transformed by the renewing of your mind, that you may prove what is that good and acceptable and perfect will of God."**
>
> ~Romans 12:2, NKJV

By renewing our minds, God tells us that we will prove His

- ✓ good,
- ✓ acceptable,
- ✓ and perfect
- ✓ will!

Praise God!

Here, God is telling us to prove Him! Notice He does not say that we will prove His will by crying out to Him daily, but by renewing our minds daily!

If you were thinking of crying yourself to sleep tonight, renew your mind instead. By reading God's perspective, you prove His will for your life!

You may be thinking to yourself, "How do I know what God's will is for my life? Finding out God's perspective, or His Word, is mysterious. After all, He does work in mysterious ways.

"How will I know what God's perspective is for my life specifically?"

I will answer this question using God's Word, so you know it is not my opinion. Remember, God's Word *is* God's will.

God's will *is* God's perspective.

The Bible says:

> **"This commandment that I'm commanding you today isn't too much for you, it's not out of your reach. It's not on a high mountain – you don't have to get mountaineers to climb the peak and bring it down to your level and explain it before you can live it. And it's not across the ocean – you don't have the send sailors out to get it, bring it back, and then explain it before you can live it. No. The word is right here and now – as near as the tongue in your mouth, as near as the heart in your chest. Just do it!"**
>
> ~Deuteronomy 30:11-14

According to the Word of God, it is right here with you.

Not mysterious.

Right here and easy to follow.

He will cause His will to manifest in your life.

To manifest something is to show or demonstrate it plainly; to reveal.

That is exactly what you want to happen with God's will!

You want to experience His promises!

This is the way it will happen.

You have God's Word on that.

The Bible says:

> **"The person who knows my commandments and keeps them, that's who loves me. And the person who loves me will be loved by my Father, and I will love him and make myself *plain* to him."**
> ~John 14:21, Emphasis mine

When you start to doubt whether God loves you, look at the above scripture as God's perspective for your life.

Think to yourself:
"He *does* love me and, because I know and do His commandments, He will make Himself plain to me. He will manifest His promises to me."

Think this every time you begin to doubt Him!

Again, this is how you renew your mind.

Renew your mind daily,

and as you do this,

your actions

become in sync with the Word of God.

When you look at a situation through God's perspective, you train your mind to respond to God, not to your circumstances!

This takes real training.

Using the example of feeling alone, you would respond according to God's perspective.

His perspective is that He is with you.

In this scenario, you would act as though you were not alone.

You would carry out your day as though God was right there with you in the flesh, as to not feel alone.

The Bible says:

> **"For we walk by faith, not by sight."**
> ~2 Corinthians 5:7, NKJV

Getting God's perspective on your situation and acting on it is how you physically "walk by faith, not by sight."

You are on your way to victory!

THIRD STEP
BELIEVE IN YOUR HEART

Praise the Lord!
I will praise the Lord with my whole heart...
Psalm 111:1 (NKJV)

In prayer it is better to have a heart without words
than words without a heart.

John Bunyan

Victory

According to the Bible, believing in your heart is another key role in the process to experience victory.

Romans 10:9 contains this statement:

"... believe in your heart ..."

Believe in your *heart*.

Here, in this very short phrase within this scripture, God is giving us another command.

He is not only telling us to believe, but He is telling us where to believe – in our hearts!

The term *heart* is the Greek word *kardia.*

The Strong's Concordance reveals the term kardia means:

> **the center and seat of spiritual life; the soul, as it is the fountain and seat of the thoughts, passions, desires, appetites, affections, purposes, endeavors.**

The heart is the center of our spiritual life!

God wants us to believe, at the center of our spiritual life.

This sounds extremely important. And if you are serious about experiencing victory, you are probably wondering how to believe in your heart.

This term "believe in your heart" refers to faith.

The Bible says:

> **"Faith is the realization of things hoped for; the confidence of things not seen."**
>
> ~Hebrews 11:1, NKJV

Realization means coming to understand something clearly and distinctly. Therefore, you must have faith in God's Word in order for you to believe in your heart. Faith is the ingredient to obtaining manifestation of the Word of God.

In fact, as you renew your mind, faith comes! Faith is when you realize that what you were hoping for in God's Word is actually true! It is the moment when your spirit and flesh together realize God's Word is true. And at that moment, that is when the manifestation comes!

Again, let me give you scripture to prove this, because I do not want you to think this is merely my opinion.

The Bible says:

> **"So then faith comes by hearing and hearing by the word of God."**
>
> ~Romans 10:17, NKJV

Faith comes by hearing the Word of God *continuously*.

Faith does not come by *having heard* the Word of God. It is similar to renewing your mind – it must be continuous.

Therefore, you must continuously hear the Word of God. As you do this, faith comes. Once faith arrives, that is when your heart believes!

Praise God!

And once your heart believes, God's Word is ready to manifest in the flesh! This is where you wanted it in the first place.

The key to this step, believing in your heart, is to be completely honest with God at all times. Even though you are a Christian, most likely you do *not* believe in your heart *all* of the things of God.

And it is important to be honest so that you will know where you are in order to help you get to where you want to be.

Let us use another example.

Let us say you have an illness in your body.

You search for God's perspective on your situation.

You then find this following piece of scripture referring to Jesus.

> **"...He took the punishment, and that made us whole. Through His bruises we get healed."**
>
> ~Isaiah 53:5

And now you know God's perspective on your situation!

You are healed!

Jesus was bruised, and when that happened, you were healed.

Probably, at this moment, you do not believe this. You feel your sick body, and you read the doctor's report. But, if you continue to hear this scripture over and over until it sinks in, faith will come to you!

Once faith arrives, you will believe in your heart that you are healed.

When you believe in your heart that you are healed, the healing that was yours in the spirit realm becomes manifest in your flesh! And, at the very moment, your body receives the healing that Jesus died for you to have!

Praise God!

Notice something very important here.

God had already healed you in the spirit realm when Jesus was bruised. You were already healed before you believed, but the *manifestation* of the healing took place when you believed.

This is why it is vital to understand our role in this process of experiencing victory. Being ignorant of the Word might have you have sitting around saying things like, "Well, this must be God's will for me. He must want me to come on home." And all the while, the devil laughs knowing that you are healed, but because you do not believe it or because you did not know the Word, you will die from the sickness.

The devil wants you dead.

Sound familiar?

The devil comes to

- ✓ steal,
- ✓ to kill,
- ✓ and to destroy.

More importantly, do you recognize that if you do not read the Word, renew your mind, and believe in your heart, that in this example, you would have most likely died from the disease unless the doctor had a cure?

Why put your life in the hands of a doctor, who is a fallible human being, when you can place your life in the hands of God, Creator and Sustainer of all life?

The Bible says:

> **"...God is strong, and He wants you strong. So take everything the Master has set out for you, well-made weapons of the best materials. And put them to use so you will be able to stand up to everything the Devil throws your way. This is no afternoon athletic contest that we'll walk away from and forget about in a couple of hours. This is for keeps, a life-or-death fight to the finish against the Devil and all his angels."**
> ~Ephesians 6:10-12

This must be the fight many Christians are losing – the ones spoken of in Hosea 4:6.

Do not be among those who will lose this fight.

Victory

We have been destined to win this fight, because of God's will.

However, if you fail to know the Word of God *and* do it, you will lose.

Do not forget God's warning in Hosea, that some of His people (Christians) will be destroyed because they lack knowledge.

This scripture is proof that God does not want you defeated in any way in your life. So if you are and you believe it is God's will for you, you are being deceived!

You are being lied to by the father of lies!

Stop believing the devil!

God wants you

- ✓ strong,
- ✓ Healed,
- ✓ and successful.

The Bible says:

> **"So, what do you think? With God on our side like this, how can we lose? If God didn't hesitate to put everything on the line for us, embracing our condition and exposing himself to the worst by sending his own Son, is there anything else he wouldn't gladly and freely do for us? And who would dare tangle with God by messing with one of God's chosen? Who would dare even to point a finger? The One who died for us—who was raised to life for us!—is in the presence of God at**

this very moment sticking up for us. Do you think anyone is going to be able to drive a wedge between us and Christ's love for us? There is no way! Not trouble, not hard times, not hatred, not hunger, not homelessness, not bullying threats, not backstabbing, not even the worst sins listed in Scripture:

'They kill us in cold blood because they hate you. We're sitting ducks; they pick us off one by one.'

None of this fazes us because Jesus loves us. I'm absolutely convinced that nothing—nothing living or dead, angelic or demonic, today or tomorrow, high or low, thinkable or unthinkable—absolutely nothing can get between us and God's love because of the way that Jesus our Master has embraced us."

~Romans 8:31-39

If you ever start to believe anything other than that, start to read God's Word over and over until faith comes!

You need faith to come so that you will believe in your heart.

Amen.

Victory

FOURTH STEP
CONFESS WITH YOUR MOUTH

It's your heart, not the dictionary that gives meaning to your words.
Matthew 12:34

I have found that there are three stages in every great work of God: first, it is impossible, then it is difficult, then it is done.
Hudson Taylor

Victory

What you say is an indication of what is in your heart. Whatever is in the center of your spiritual life is what will come out of your mouth. That is why you must first believe in your heart before you will experience the victory that God has given you.

When you speak, that should be the trigger – or point of contact – of your faith! Jesus spoke to the storm. Instantly, the storm responded as Jesus wanted.

Why?

Why so quickly?

Because Jesus was renewing His mind, He believed in His heart (His center), so when He spoke – poof! Instantly, it was so! We are designed the same way!

You may be thinking to yourself, "Well, I speak to my troubles all the time and it is has not ever been instantly solved. Why?" This is because one of the steps in the process has not yet been completed in you. Either you are not renewing your mind, or you do not yet believe in your heart.

This is because if you are renewing your mind, and you believe in your heart, then the moment you speak – poof! It will be done!

Jesus says:

> **"... The simple truth is that if you had a mere kernel of faith, a poppy seed, say, you would tell this mountain, "Move!" and it would move. There is nothing you wouldn't be able to tackle."**
>
> ~Matthew 17:20

This is why it is important to understand not only what to do, but *how* to do it. If I only told you the process without providing you with the information on how to achieve it, it would be extremely cruel.

It would create a religious mind set in you and you would say to yourself, "I am blessed going in and blessed going out" throughout the day and never experience the victory!

This is because speaking is not what allows you to experience victory, but it is speaking what you believe in your heart while you are renewing your mind that brings the victory experience to you.

This entire process works together to bring you the promises.

Speak!
The Bible says:

> **"Words satisfy the mind as much as fruit does the stomach; good talk is as**

gratifying as a good harvest. Words kill, words give life; they're either poison or fruit – you choose."

~Proverbs 18:20-21

This is why it is best to pray aloud whenever you can.

Do not stop speaking God's Word.

There is great power in His Word. While you are doing the process, speak! Speak His Word all the time.

The Bible says:

> **"Just as rain and snow descend from the skies and don't go back until they've watered the earth, doing their work of making things grow and blossom, producing seed for farmers and food for the hungry, so will the words that come out of my mouth not come back empty handed."**

~Isaiah 55:10-11

The Bible also says:

> **"...you His angels, who excel in strength, who do His word, heeding the voice of His word. It has been stated over and over again that God spoke life into creation. We marvel saying, "Wow" to ourselves."**

~Psalm 103:20

However, we fail to make the connection between God and us.

We are His creation!

His children!

We are made in His image and we reflect His nature!

He spoke and instantly things were done. This was able to happen because He knows Himself; He knows His power, therefore He has done the process too! The process reminds us all to gain knowledge of God and His Word, because we will then realize who we are, what we are entitled to, and understand our role on this planet.

The more you speak,

the more you will hear,

and faith will come!

This is real.

This is not a magic act or will power.

It is the Power of God's will!

Do not underestimate the power of your speech.

It may seem as the least of the process, but without speaking it, the fulfillment of the promise will not manifest.

Jesus did not *think* to the storm;

He spoke to it!

God did not *think* creation; He spoke it! The speech is the method in which God's power is released. This is similar to when a believer touches you on the forehead in prayer – it is the point of contact.

I purposely chose not to focus on what happens we speak words that are not of God, because I do not want that to become your focus. Focus only on speaking what God speaks.

When you consult God as to His perspective, continue to renew your mind, you will naturally start talking like God.

Wow!

You start to live out who you truly are and were meant to be –

God's children!

Amen.

EPILOGUE
BEING HONEST WITH YOURSELF

Yes. I'm full of myself—after all, I've spent a long time in sin's prison. What I don't understand about myself is that I decide one way, but then I act another, doing things I absolutely despise.

Romans 7:15

I want to be a giant for God

Billy Sunday

Victory

By this point, you have almost finished this book and I have two honest questions for you: Have you read something in these pages you had not known before?

Was this the first book you ever read that informed you on the promises of God and then laid out a plan to achieve it?

I have another honest question before I get into this final chapter:

If you have read a book in the past that informed you on God's promises, have you obtained any of them?

I ask these questions, because I want you to be honest

- ✓ with me,
- ✓ with God,
- ✓ and with yourself.

Chances are that you have read plenty of books that have revealed God's Word to you.

Also, chances are that most of the same problems that you had while you read the other books are still in your life today. I do not mention this to put you on the defensive, but to clearly show you that God does not transform your life by reading books.

God uses books and His Words to help you make the choice to choose life instead of death. Please make the *decision* to choose life in order for God to make manifest His promises to you.

Do not merely read this book and say, "That was a nice book." Rather, say, "Thank you God for not giving up on me. Thank you for bringing your Word to me through various people until I got it." Once you say that, please start the process to experiencing victory today!

Glory to God!

The Bible says:

> **"…'I know that all God's commands are spiritual, but I'm not. Isn't this also your experience?' Yes. I'm full of myself — after all, I've spent a long time in sin's prison. What I don't understand about myself is that I decide one way, but then I act another, doing things I absolutely despise. So if I can't be trusted to figure out what is best for myself and then do it, it becomes obvious that God's command is necessary.**
>
> **But I need something more!**

For if I know the law but still can't keep it, and if the power of sin within me keeps sabotaging my best intentions, I obviously need help! I realize that I don't have what it takes. I can will it, but I can't do it. I decide to do good, but I don't really do it. I decide not to do bad, but then I do it anyway.

My decisions, such as they are, don't result in actions. Something has gone wrong deep within me and gets the better of me every time. It happens so regularly that it's predictable. The moment I decide to do good, sin is there to trip me up. I truly delight in God's commands, but it's pretty obvious that not all of me joins in that delight.

Parts of me covertly rebel, and just when I least expect it, they take charge. I've tried everything and nothing helps. I'm at the end of my rope. Is there no one who can do anything for me? Isn't that the real question? The answer, thank God, is that Jesus Christ can and does. He acted to set things right in this life of contradictions where I want to serve God with all my heart and mind, but am pulled by the influence of sin to do something totally different."

~Romans 7:13-25

I have read through the Word many times, and have only now found this passage of scripture in one of my favorite books in the New Testament!
Praise God!

Victory

This passage is relating to our new selves operating in our old bodies away from sin.

This applies to the process of experiencing victory through the Word of God.

Too many times, we only

- ✓ read the books,
- ✓ hear the sermons,
- ✓ pray to God,

and then

nothing.

Nothing happens.

We fail to *implement* the Word in our lives, but at the same time, we honestly ask God why we are not living out the promises in His Word?

Do you see the irony?

Do not let this remain to be your routine in life:

that you *hear*, but fail to *do*.

This is why Jesus left us a Helper –

The Holy Spirit!

Did you ever wonder why He left Him?

He knew we would need Him!

Obtaining the victory promised in God's Word is not easy, but it is obtainable. Do not let the process frustrate you into thinking that it will not happen. Do not think that the promises in the Word are only for the "cream of the crop" Christians!

Please remember that sin is the transgression of the law. Therefore, when we fail to *do* God's Word, we are in sin.

If you *remain* poor, you are in sin. You would be in sin because it is impossible to act on God's Word, in the area of finances, and remain poor.

If you *remain* sick, you are in sin.

You would be in sin because it is impossible to act on God's Word, in the area of healing, and remain sick.

You may be thinking, "Michael, that is pretty harsh." It may be harsh, but it is the truth of God's Word. God said that His Word will not return back to Him empty handed.

Therefore, if you

- ✓ renew your mind,
- ✓ believe in your heart,
- ✓ and confess with your mouth

that, "By Jesus' stripes, I'm healed," you will be!

Simple as that – you will be!

Remember, the Word says that God is not a man that He should lie. Continue to study the Word of God until faith comes to you.

This is the spiritual battle we have been warned about! This is the good fight of faith! This is it! Right here, right now.

What decision will you make?

Will you, with the help of the Holy Spirit, implement God's Word in your life today?

Or, as Paul wrote in Romans, continue to allow sin to sabotage your best intentions to

- ✓ be rich.
- ✓ be healthy.
- ✓ have self-esteem.

God says:

> **"I call heaven and earth as witnesses today against you, that I have set before you life and death, blessing and cursing; therefore choose life, that both you and your descendants may live…"**
>
> ~Deuteronomy 30:19

Will you choose blessings,

or cursings?

God said we get to choose!

So choose wisely.
As I am writing this, I can hardly sit still – I am so excited.

I am so full of the Spirit!

It is so radical to think that blessings are just one choice away. It is so radical to really, truly, authentically, believe the Bible!

Wow!

How radical!

This is what Jesus allowed Himself to be murdered for!

For us!

To come to the knowledge of God and of ourselves!

That is why Jesus was so disappointed and saddened by Peter losing his faith while he walked on the water (Matthew 14:22-33).

Jesus was disappointed because He knew Peter was more than capable of doing it! It is the same reason that when Jesus would heal the sick, He would let them know it was accomplished because of *their* faith (Matthew 9:22).

In effect Jesus would tell those who were sick (and I am paraphrasing), "Your faith did it. Don't look at me – you allowed the blessing on you!"

Jesus is saying that to you, the reader, right now. He is saying (I am paraphrasing again), "I have placed the options before you. You pick. This means that you choose the direction your life takes. It is true that I have a desired route for you, but it is in your hands. Please choose life. I purchased that life for you with my blood."

The bottom line is you must be honest with yourself and determine what it is that you truly want from God.

Your *true* desires.

For example, if you truly wanted to be rich, according to the Bible standards, you would

- ✓ seek out the scriptures,

- ✓ study them,
- ✓ implement the process
- ✓ and receive the promise.

The process is difficult and not everyone will carry it out.

Why?

And before you say, "The process is too hard," think of how hard it is to remain at a job that you hate while earning an income that you despise more. The real reason you may decide not to follow through on the process is because you want something *else*.

You simply want the stuff: the house, car, vacations, clothing, etc. The desire for material gain will take you away from the process.

Ironically, following through on the process will bring the material goods to you! Let us use a financial example of this principle. Let us say you tell yourself, "I want to be rich in order to afford the house of my dreams."

Therefore, you want the house, not necessarily the money. In this scenario, you begin the process of finding all the scriptures that relate to your desire.
However, because you do not truly want to be rich, but rather accumulate the things that rich people have, you decide to skip the scriptures on being a good steward over your finances and focus more on the "name it and claim it scriptures."

After a few days of prayer without seeing any result, you decide to quit the process. You will quit when you see another possible way of getting that house.

Perhaps by financing it through some new financing promotion which allows you to get the house you want, but at an extremely high cost - more than you can comfortably afford. You will get the house anyway, because you wanted the house, not the wealth.

Do you see the difference between wanting to be rich and wanting material possessions? If you line up your desires to the will of God, you will experience the promises. God wants you to be rich (Psalm 35:27). Being wealthy will bring you the house, while having the house first may drive away your wealth.

Therefore, ensure that the desires that you are seeking are from God and those desires shall be made manifest in your life!

What is it that you really want in your life?

If you find you want the stuff, that is fine, but begin to pursue the Word first and desire to obtain the promises of God, and the house will come!

God promises that!

Choose to recite those "name it and claim it" scriptures, but also do the Word of God regarding being a good steward over your finances, by bringing God His tithes, giving offerings, and managing your money well.

Do it all.

Do not merely pick and choose.

God will not be manipulated.

I know this is a small book, but please allow it to reach you where you are and to help point you in the direction that you really want to go.

Please do not simply add this book to a growing collection of "name it and claim it" books, and say, "That was a great book."

Please, do not let it end during this chapter.

- ✓ Please reread this book,
- ✓ study the Word,
- ✓ start the process,
- ✓ and listen to sermons

that will help you through the process, and start to put yourself around people who will help edify you.

You might be thinking to yourself that if this book really contained the steps necessary for any and all believers to experience victory, then why isn't everyone experiencing victory now?

The answer is two fold.

For one, the victory isn't automatic. The will of God does not always manifest in the believer's life. I am not saying that the will of God isn't always *true*. I said it does not always *manifest*. There is a very important distinction that must be made.

The manifestation requires your *faith in action*. God's word, or will, has a role for both parties involved in the transaction – 1) God and 2) you. It is God's job that He provides the promise. It is your job to bring the promise to fruition. You accomplish this by building up your faith and walking it out. This is the main reason believers never experience consistent victory in their lives.

Second, the role of you, the believer, is uncomfortable and inconvenient.

Notice I did not say the believer's role is hard or too heavy to carry out. I said it's uncomfortable and inconvenient.

Jesus says:

> **"For my yoke is easy to bear, and the burden I give you is light."**
> ~Matthew 11:30, NLT

The yoke, or the proper way of living, is easy, but uncomfortable. His burden, or commands, He gives are light, but inconvenient.

This is the other reason why so few believers experience the victorious life He promised us!

Somewhere along the line believers thought that Jesus promised us everything *without any requirements*.

This is not the case.

From His own lips, He says that His yoke is easy, not that there isn't a yoke. He says His burden is light, not that it's non-existent. Let us not miss these distinctions.

If you are willing to be uncomfortable and inconvenienced for a short while, you will experience victory all the time.

For example, you are sick and you want to experience victory over the sickness. When you turn to God's word, He says you're healed by His stripes! Two things must happen: you must have sufficient faith and must "walk by faith" until it manifests. Faith comes by hearing and hearing, so you must confess "I am healed." That's inconvenient, because you have to bridle your tongue from confessing your sickness because you don't yet believe it. Then you must go on with your day as though you are healed – that's uncomfortable, because your body is sick!

But if you do that consistently, you will strengthen your faith and it will cause the healing to manifest. It's the same when you go for a workout at the gym. As you continually do the workout routine (as though you're already in shape), you manifest being in shape. It works the same in the Kingdom of God.

Victory

Lastly, rid yourself of those who pull you down instead of lifting you up.

Allow this book to be the one that finally has you "up and running!"

I pray that in all of your endeavors, may God manifest Himself to you!

I'd like to end with this prayer I found in <u>Praying God's Word</u> by Beth Moore

Pray this prayer while you continue in this process:

> **Lord God, I do not understand what I do. For what I want to do I do not do, but what I hate to do. Sin is living in me. I know that nothing good lives in me, that is, in my sinful nature. For I have the desire to do what is good, but I cannot carry it out. For what I do is not the good I want to do; no, the evil I do not want to do – this I keep on doing. So I find this law at work: When I want to do good, evil is right there with me. (Rom. 7:15-21) Lord God, in my inner being I delight in Your law; but I see another law at work in the members of my body, waging war against the law of my mind and making me a prisoner of the law of sin at work within my members. How wretched I am! Who will rescue me from this body of death? Thanks be to God – through Jesus Christ our Lord! (Rom. 7:22-25)**
>
> **Lord, You sent Your Son to rescue me from this body of death! Set me free to new life in You, Lord. I do not have to be**

a prisoner to sin. Please help me understand that the battle that rages over my body originates in my mind. Please help me to surrender my mind to You and to Your truth.

MAY THE PROMISES OF GOD MANIFEST IN YOUR LIFE!

THANK YOU FOR READING THIS BOOK.

I pray God used it to change your life. If you have not yet made Jesus, the Christ, the Lord and Savior of your life, then please pray the following life-changing prayer:

> Almighty Father,
>
> I know and acknowledge that I am a sinner. I repent, right now, of all my sins, and I am asking you to forgive me. You said in your Word, "Whosoever shall call upon the name of the Lord shall be saved" (Romans 10:13). And so, I am calling on the name of your Son, Jesus, to be my Savior. You also said, ". . . if you confess with your mouth, 'Jesus is Lord,' and believe in your heart that God raised him from the dead, you will be saved" (Romans 10:9). I believe with my heart that Jesus died for my sins and was raised from the dead so that I may have eternal life. I confess Him, right now, as my Lord. In the name of Jesus I submit this prayer. Amen.

Now that you have prayed the prayer of salvation, know that you have made the best decision one can make. I encourage you to seek out a Christ-centered, God-fearing, Bible-believing church to cultivate your new found faith.

BE VICTORIOUS!

Teaching Resources from Michael Jefferson

Eliminating Pride

Experience

Freedom

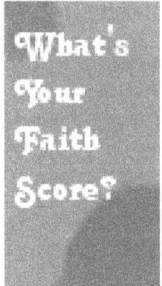
What's Your Faith Score?

Faith the Heals

Fun!

Seek First Thy Kingdom?

Fruit of the Spirit

How to Study the Bible

For more teaching resources, visit
WWW.JOYFORCHRIST.ORG

ABOUT THE AUTHOR

Michael L. Jefferson inspires great joy and enthusiasm while revealing the victory-filled knowledge of God's Word, encouraging people to embrace their reconciled life in Christ. Through Joy for Christ Ministries, his teaching ministry, he also produces sermons and the daily podcast, VICTORY. From 2007 to 2008, Michael also hosted and produced VICTORY TV, the television outreach arm of his teaching ministry. Michael resides in Rhode Island where he teaches at Legions of Christ Empowerment Center. He developed the discipleship curriculum for the ministry leaders and mentors a group of young men in their walk with Christ.

www.ingramcontent.com/pod-product-compliance
Lightning Source LLC
Chambersburg PA
CBHW031417040426

42444CB00005B/614